Boots Randolph
Stompin' at the Savoy

B♭ TENOR SAXOPHONE/TRUMPET

E♭ ALTO SAXOPHONE

To access audio visit:
www.halleonard.com/mylibrary

Enter Code
6629-7216-5435-6938

ISBN 978-1-59615-746-0

EXCLUSIVELY DISTRIBUTED BY

7777 W. BLUEMOUND RD. P.O. BOX 13819 MILWAUKEE, WI 53213

Visit Hal Leonard Online at
www.halleonard.com

From the Producer . . .

I feel very blessed to have known Boots Randolph for twenty-five years. I first met him when my father, the late comedian Ralph Smith, was recording a comedy album at Boots' legendary Printer's Alley nightclub in 1980. I remember being blown away by Boots and his band. Later that year Fred Foster hired me to play bass on Boots' last project for Monument Records, *Dedication*. Fast forward to 1996 – I had just moved back to Nashville after a stint in France. An opportunity to "sub" on Boots' band one night led to him offering me the job full-time, and I have no intention of ever leaving! I have had the pleasure of producing several records on Boots through the last ten years, and this latest offering is something truly special for all of us involved in the making of it. Through the years, Boots has always had a "concept" in mind when he began a new project. Together, we have done a project of Nashville classic recordings, a Christmas project, and a gospel project. Boots and I had talked many late nights driving back to Nashville about a new project – we just never seemed to come up with a concept that we were as enthused about after a good night's sleep. One day driving to Boots' home to talk about recording, it hit me. Boots is 78 years old, he has cut nearly fifty albums, he is playing as well as he has ever played – who needs a concept? Let's just record a group of Boots' favorite songs, songs he had never recorded previously. Well, there's a concept for you.

We discussed a few titles, and made plans to get together at the studio on a Saturday to "see if anything would happen." Well, did it ever. The first session opened a floodgate, and we soon had fourteen songs that we really wanted to record – and that's what we did. Boots is fond of calling great standards "evergreens," and that is a wonderful description of the titles represented here. It seems like the last few years have produced a glut of artists recording the great standards, so what could we bring to the table that would be new and unique? The answer is in the artist himself. Boots is one of the most unique instrumentalists in the history of modern music. He has proven to be a special interpreter of great melodies. He has proven to be a master of the saxophone in many genres, from country to blues, to pop, to swinging jazz. He possesses one if the most imitated and respected "tones" in the business. On every song in this collection, you will hear a master musician deliver the melody in a way that only Boots can, and you will hear the most adventurous solos that Boots has recorded to date. His legion of fans will get a huge dose of Boots' horn on this project, with no apologies. Our drummer, Ray Von Rotz, repeatedly reminded us all that we didn't need to cheat the boss out of any choruses on these songs, and I am so thrilled that we didn't. We tackled some very difficult music, both harmonically and technically.

I don't think I have ever heard a fan talk to Boots without asking him if he has a favorite sax player. They want to know who his influences are, and why he became the sax player he is today. Boots always mentions the huge names in the jazz sax world, players like Ben Webster, Coleman Hawkins, Lester Young, and Charlie Parker. However, he never fails to mention a man named Don Byas. I had heard Byas mentioned by a lot of jazz experts, but was not too familiar with his work. As we started picking material for this project, Boots brought me a copy of Don Byas playing a great old song called "Candy." I was floored. First of all, Byas plays the song brilliantly. His time is incredible. His note choice is flawless. His tone is incredibly "contemporary" for his time period. And as a huge fan of Boots, I suddenly put part of the puzzle together. A great musician is a product of his influences, and with his own stamp of creativity becomes a unique artist. Well, thank you, Mr. Byas, for what you brought to the table! I have been lucky enough to have worked with and become friends of many of the top sax players in music today. Bill Evans, the great sax player from Miles Davis's 1980's supergroups came to Nashville to do a record. We have been friends for many years, and he knew that I was working with Boots. He asked if Boots would come in and do a duet with him. One of the first sax players his parents exposed him to at a young age was Boots, and he has been a huge fan for many years. We had great fun making that duet. Kirk Whalum might possibly be the most respected tenor sax player in the current crop of jazz stars. He is a good friend of mine, and has actually told me that one of the reasons he made the move to Nashville years back was "to breathe the same air that Boots did." So, in the same way that these young musicians revere Boots, Boots is giving something back on this record. Boots loves these songs and this is his gift to the listeners.

The band on this record is very special, too. Ray Von Rotz has been with Boots well over twenty years. A great musician, and versatile drummer, Ray found his niche with Boots. Nobody plays this material like Ray. He never ceases to be musical at any tempo or style. Steve Willets joined the band five years ago, and what a find he turned out to be. Steve is not only a tremendous pianist, but he is a fabulous singer, and an encyclopedia of the jazz idiom. He brings incredible energy to the stage and studio. His "time" is just wonderful and he is a great arranger. Roddy Smith is the guitarist on the project. He has been on several of Boots' projects in the past, and began performing live with the group earlier this year. He plays great tasty rhythm as well as some beautiful, bluesy, soulful solos on the record. I played the bass on the record, as I also do on Boots' live shows. His music never ceases to challenge me. I have to admit, I spend most of my time playing Boots' music with a smile on my face. I know that working with him is the highest honor I could have as a player. He always brings his "A game," as Tiger Woods says. He is a true example of being a pro musician. We can't wait to start the next record!

- Tim Smith

4276

CONTENTS

B♭ TENOR SAXOPHONE/TRUMPET

MMO 4276

Bb Instrument

Stompin' at the Savoy

Words by Andy Razaf
Music by Benny Goodman, Edgar Sampson and Chick Webb

♩ = 140

Bb Tenor Sax

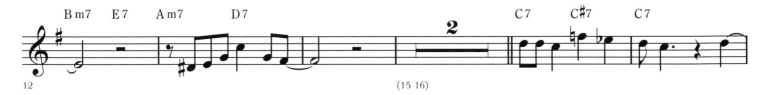

Cry Me a River

Words and Music by
Arthur Hamilton

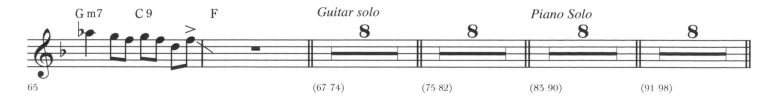

L-O-V-E

Words and Music by
Bert Kaempfert and Milt Gabler

MMO 4276

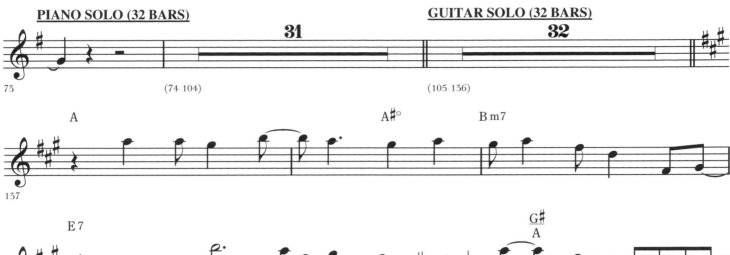

PIANO SOLO (32 BARS)   GUITAR SOLO (32 BARS)

Bb Instrument

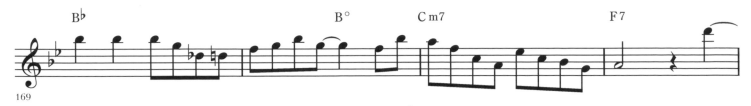

169

173

177

181

184

187

190

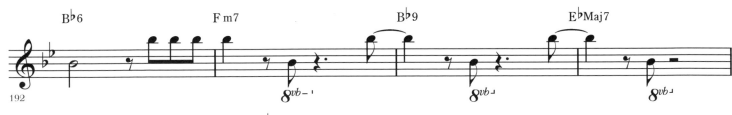

192

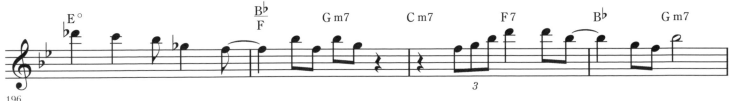

196

You'll Never Know

Words and Music by
Bert Kaempfert and Milt Gabler

I'll Walk Alone

from the Motion Picture FOLLOW THE BOYS
from WITH A SONG IN MY HEART

Lyric by Sammy Cahn
Music by Jule Styne

As Time Goes By

from the Warner Bros. motion picture CASABLANCA

Words and Music by
Herman Hupfield

Red Sails in the Sunset

Words by Jimmy Kennedy
Music by Hugh Williams (Will Grosz)

Bb Tenor Sax

Embraceable You

(from "Girl Crazy")

Music and Lyrics by
George and Ira Gershwin

Bb Tenor Sax

Eb ALTO SAXOPHONE

Stompin' at the Savoy

Words by Andy Razaf
Music by Benny Goodman, Edgar Sampson and Chick Webb

Cry Me a River

Words and Music by
Arthur Hamilton

Eb Instrument

L-O-V-E

Words and Music by
Bert Kaempfert and Milt Gabler

MMO 4276

Eb Instrument

You'll Never Know

Lyrics by Max Gordon
Music by Harry Warren

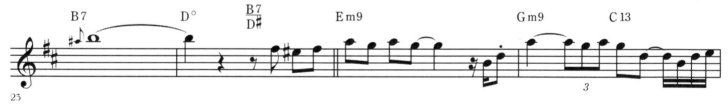

I'll Walk Alone

from the Motion Picture FOLLOW THE BOYS
from WITH A SONG IN MY HEART

Lyric by Sammy Cahn
Music by Jule Styne

As Time Goes By

from the Warner Bros. motion picture CASABLANCA

Words and Music by
Herman Hupfield

Red Sails in the Sunset

Words by Jimmy Kennedy
Music by Hugh Williams (Will Grosz)

Embraceable You

Music and Lyrics by
George and Ira Gershwin

Eb Alto Sax

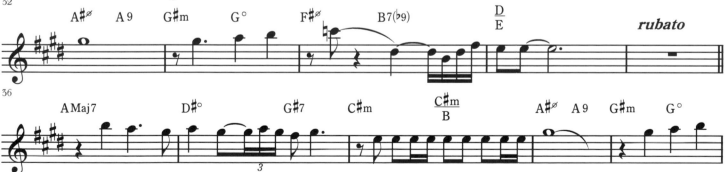
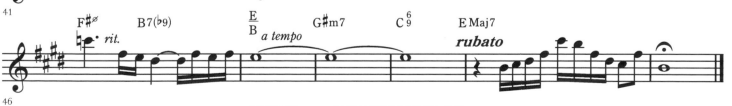

ADVANCED ALTO SAX SOLOS – VOLUME 1

Performed by Paul Brodie, alto saxophone
Accompaniment: Antonin Kubalek, piano

Virtuoso Paul Brodie introduces you to the world of advanced alto sax solos with this wide-ranging collection. Contains performance suggestions and Mr. Brodie's incredible interpretations to help you achieve greatness! Includes a printed music score containing the solo part, annotated with performance suggestions; and access to professional recordings with complete versions (with soloist) followed by piano accompaniments to each piece, minus the soloist. Includes works by Vivaldi, Jacob, Whitney, and Benson.

00400602 Book/Online Audio...$14.99

ADVANCED ALTO SAX SOLOS – VOLUME 2

Performed by Vincent Abato, alto saxophone
Accompaniment: Harriet Wingreen, piano

Listen as extraordinary virtuoso Vincent Abato of the Metropolitan Opera Orchestra takes you further into the advanced repertoire with these spectacular sax selections. Listen to his masterful interpretations, examine his performance suggestions, then you step in and make magic with Harriet Wingreen, legendary piano accompanist for the New York Philharmonic. Includes: Schubert "The Bee," Rabaud "Solo de Concours," and Creston "Sonata, Op. 19" 2nd and 3rd movements. Includes a printed music score containing the solo part, annotated with performance suggestions; and tracks with complete versions (with soloist) followed by piano accompaniments to each piece, minus the soloist.

00400603 Book/Online Audio $14.99

PLAY THE MUSIC OF BURT BACHARACH
ALTO OR TENOR SAXOPHONE

Along with lyricist Hal David, Burt Bacharach penned some of the best pop songs and standards of all time. These superb collections let solo instrumentalists play along with: Alfie • Blue on Blue • Do You Know the Way to San Jose • I Say a Little Prayer • Magic Moments • This Guy's in Love with You • Walk on By • What the World Needs Now • The Windows of the World • and Wives and Lovers.

00400657 Book/Online Audio $19.99

BOSSA, BONFÁ & BLACK ORPHEUS FOR TENOR SAXOPHONE – A TRIBUTE TO STAN GETZ
TENOR SAXOPHONE

featuring Glenn Zottola

Original transcriptions for you to perform! The bossa novas that swept the world in 1950 created a whole new set of songs to equal the great standards of the '20s, '30s and '40s by Gershwin, Porter, Arlen, Berlin, Kern and Rodgers. This collection for tenor sax is a tribute to the great Stan Getz and includes: Black Orpheus • Girl from Ipanema • Gentle Rain • One Note Samba • Once I Loved • Dindi • Baubles, Bangles and Beads • Meditation • Triste • I Concentrate on You • Samba de Orfeu.

00124387 Book/Online Audio..$14.99

CLASSIC STANDARDS FOR ALTO SAXOPHONE
A TRIBUTE TO JOHNNY HODGES

featuring Bob Wilber

Ten classic standards are presented in this book as they were arranged for the Neal Hefti String Orchestra in 1954, including: Yesterdays • Laura • What's New? • Blue Moon • Can't Help Lovin' Dat Man • Embraceable You • Willow Weep for Me • Memories of You • Smoke Gets in Your Eyes • Stardust. Bob Wilber performs the songs on the provided CD on soprano saxophone, although they are translated for alto saxophone.

00131389 Book/CD Pack...$14.99

EASY JAZZ DUETS FOR 2 ALTO SAXOPHONES AND RHYTHM SECTION

Performed by Hal McKusick, alto saxophone
Accompaniment: The Benny Goodman Rhythm Section:
George Duvivier, bass; Bobby Donaldson, drums

This great collection of jazz duets gives you the opportunity to accompany saxophonist Hal McKusick and the Benny Goodman Rhythm Section. Suitable for beginning players, all the selections are great fun. This album allows you to play either duet part. Includes printed musical score with access to online audio tracks: you hear both parts played in stereo, then each duet is repeated with the first part omitted and then the second part, so you can play along.

00400480 Book/Online Audio...$14.99

FROM DIXIE TO SWING
CLARINET OR SOPRANO SAX

Performed by Kenny Davern, clarinet
Accompaniment: Kenny Davern, clarinet & soprano sax; 'Doc' Cheatham, trumpet; Vic Dickenson, trombone; Dick Wellstood, piano; George Duvivier, bass; Gus Johnson Jr., drums

Such jazz legends as Dick Wellstood, Alphonse 'Doc' Cheatham and George Duvivier and more back you up in this amazing collection of New York-style Dixieland standards. After the break-up of the big-band era around 1950, many of the finest 'swing' or mainstream players found themselves without an outlet for their abilities and took to playing 'Dixieland' in New York clubs such as Eddie Condon's and the Metropole. And so was born a new style of Dixieland jazz minus the banjos, tubas, steamboats and magnolias! It is this version we celebrate on this album. We encourage you, the soloist, to invent counter-melodies rather than mere harmony parts. This is a music of loose weaving parts, not one of precision ensemble figures. And in short, it is one of the greatest improvisational experiences any jazz player could hope to have. Includes a printed music score and online audio access to stereo accompaniments to each piece.

00400613 Book/Online Audio $14.99

GLAZUNOV – CONCERTO IN E-FLAT MAJOR, OP. 109; VON KOCH – CONCERTO IN E-FLAT MAJOR
ALTO SAXOPHONE

Performed by Lawrence Gwozdz, alto saxophone
Accompaniment: Plovdiv Philharmonic Orchestra
Conductor: Nayden Todorov

Alexander Glazunov, one of the great masters of late Russian Romanticism, was fascinated by the saxophone and by jazz. In 1934 he wrote this beautiful saxophone concerto which has become a classic, combining romanticism with modern idioms as well. Erland von Koch's 1958 saxophone concerto is filled with experimental modern tonalities and fantastic effects for the saxophone. Both are must-haves for the serious saxophonist. Includes a printed music score; informative liner notes; and online audio featuring the concerti performed twice: first with soloist, then again with orchestral accompaniment only, minus you, the soloist. The audio is accessed online using the unique code inside each book and can be streamed or downloaded.

00400487 Book/Online Audio...$14.99